Beyond THE GAME

ATHLETES CHANGE THE WORLD

MAYA MOORE

Also by Andrew Maraniss

Strong Inside: Perry Wallace and the Collision of Race and Sports in the South

Strong Inside (Young Readers Edition): *The True Story of How Perry Wallace Broke College Basketball's Color Line*

Games of Deception: The True Story of the First U.S. Olympic Basketball Team at the 1936 Olympics in Hitler's Germany

Singled Out: The True Story of Glenn Burke

Inaugural Ballers: The True Story of the First U.S. Women's Olympic Basketball Team

Beyond THE GAME

ATHLETES CHANGE THE WORLD

MAYA MOORE

Written by Andrew Maraniss
Illustrated by DeAndra Hodge

VIKING

VIKING

An imprint of Penguin Random House LLC, New York

First published in the United States of America by Viking,
an imprint of Penguin Random House LLC, 2024

Visit us online at PenguinRandomHouse.com.

Library of Congress Cataloging-in-Publication Data is available.

ISBN 9780593526187 (hardcover)

ISBN 9780593526194 (paperback)

1st Printing

Printed in the United States of America

LSCC

Edited by Kelsey Murphy
Design by Anabeth Bostrup

Text set in Baskerville

For Eliza and Charlie —Andrew Maraniss

To my mom and my big brother, my two favorite basketball players. I'm glad we could bond over sports for once! Love, your favorite art kid —DeAndra Hodge

BEYOND THE GAME

A Note about the Series

"A life is not important except in the impact
it has on *other* lives."
—Jackie Robinson

BEYOND THE GAME tells the stories of remarkable athletes to convey lessons on empathy, justice, and social good. As a parent of elementary-school-age kids, I worry about the profound problems we are leaving for our children to solve. Even concepts as basic as truth and democracy are in peril.

It's never too early to share the stories of people who have fought against hate and injustice in all its forms. We tend to admire athletes for their strength, speed, and victories. But this series does not celebrate athletes solely for their athletic feats. Instead, it chronicles those who have used their platforms to help other people not merely by writing a check, posing for a photo, or showing up in the community for a day, but through extraordinary acts of humanitarianism.

Of course, this doesn't mean the subjects of these books are perfect or have not made—or will not make—mistakes in other areas of their lives. Athletes are human, after all.

But in a way, that's the point.

The people featured in this series are inspiring not because athletes are more important or better than anyone else, but because in revealing their humanity, they challenge the rest of us to act, too.

"Any time you have an opportunity to make a difference in this world and you don't, then you are wasting your time on this earth."

—Roberto Clemente

BEYOND THE GAME:

ATHLETES CHANGE THE WORLD

MAYA MOORE

CHAPTER ONE

EVERY MORNING WHEN three-year-old Maya Moore got out of bed, she treated the day as an opportunity for an adventure. Maya had so much energy that her mom, Kathryn, always knew where Maya was—even if she couldn't see her, she could hear her.

There went Maya, running fast, screaming loud, knocking things over, having fun. She was an energetic toddler whose motor never stopped running.

Crash, bang, boom!

A little girl like that was a handful for a single mom. Working and raising a child by herself in Jefferson City, Missouri, Kathryn desperately needed a way to keep Maya busy and find an outlet for her energy.

One day, Kathryn made a simple decision that changed Maya's life: she bought a small plastic basketball hoop and attached it to a door in their apartment.

From that day on, Maya spent hours running down the hall and shooting at her little hoop.

She fell in love with basketball.

Maya may have come into this world on June 11, 1989, but the day that basketball hoop appeared in her apartment was the day a superstar was born.

CHAPTER TWO

WHEN SHE WAS SEVEN, Maya signed up to play on her first basketball team. She was taller than all the other girls, and a better hooper than most of them, too. She had quick feet, strong arms and legs, and a sharp mind for the game. For Maya, playing basketball was as important to life as fresh air, food, and water. So when she outgrew the toy basketball hoop, her mom bought a real one and set it up in the driveway.

COMETS
14

Swish!

Maya spent hours practicing her shot. And she learned that if she bounced the ball off the curb just right, it would bounce back to her for an alley-oop dunk.

Slam!

Around this time, the Women's National Basketball Association, a professional basketball league for women, began playing games. Before the WNBA, only men had a chance to play pro basketball in the United States. It seemed like big-time hoops was only for boys—but that wasn't how Maya felt, and it wasn't how she played.

When Maya watched women in the WNBA play ball on TV, she felt like she was sitting in the front row at a magic show. She was amazed by all the players' grace, size, and speed, but her favorite was high-scoring Cynthia Cooper of the Houston Comets. Maya dreamed of being the best someday, too, so she copied Cynthia from head to toe. She dressed in red-and-blue Comets T-shirts and wore a Comets cap over her long black braids. Her uncle gave her a WNBA ball, and Maya carried it everywhere. Practicing on her hoop at home, Maya copied Cynthia's moves and imagined putting on a real WNBA uniform. She could practically feel the silky shorts and the hardwood court, smell the popcorn in the arena, and hear the roar of the crowd.

But Maya enjoyed more than just sports. She

loved eating red velvet cake, singing at the top of her lungs, hanging out with her cousins and godparents, and playing the drums. When she was ten, she washed cars to earn money to buy her own drum set. Getting her clothes drenched in soap bubbles and water was well worth the reward.

When Maya was eleven, her mom took a new job in North Carolina. It was hard for Maya to leave family in Missouri, especially her godparents, who helped raise her. But Maya packed up her basketball and her sneakers and found new places to hoop in North Carolina.

Life got harder a year later, when Maya's mom lost her job and told Maya it was time to move again. This time, they boxed up their belongings and moved to the Atlanta, Georgia, area.

Middle school can be an awkward time for any kid. For Maya, it wasn't easy. She was the new girl, she wore size-thirteen shoes, and, at six feet tall, she was taller than most of her teachers. Students at her new middle school called Maya names and picked on her.

But Maya's deep faith helped her find peace even when other kids bullied her. She believed that God puts everyone on Earth to help other people and to make the world a better place. When she thought about that, she didn't worry about the mean things kids said to her at school.

Basketball also helped keep Maya's mind off

her troubles. As a tween, she continued to show extra-special basketball talent. It was clear that her lofty basketball dreams were not far-fetched. Maybe she actually could play in college and the WNBA someday.

Even as a middle schooler, Maya—like her mom—believed that a college scholarship was a real possibility. That would be a big deal for a family that didn't have lots of money. Maya was so determined to play in college that when she wasn't shooting hoops, she wrote letters to the best coaches in America. She told them about her love for the game, her awesome stats, and her high grades in school.

One of those coaches, Geno Auriemma of the University of Connecticut, saved Maya's letter in his desk drawer. It wasn't often he got a letter from a middle schooler. He made a note to pay attention to the precocious girl from Georgia.

CHAPTER THREE

BY THE TIME Maya enrolled at Collins Hill High School near Atlanta, she was already a complete player. Like a movie star who could sing, dance, and act, Maya was a triple threat.

She was a graceful player who could float to the hoop for a layup.

Whoosh!

She was a strong player who could rebound the ball in the paint and score.

Boom!

She was a tough player who could steal the ball and lead the fast break.

Zoom!

She could even leap high into the air and dunk.

Bang!

Maya wasn't just the best player on her team. She wasn't just the best player in Georgia. She was one of the best players in the entire country, named to the All-American team her first two years of high school.

But being *one of the best* wasn't good enough for Maya.

In both of her final two years of high school, she was voted the very best player in the United States. Imagine a looooong line of all the high school basketball players in the country. How long would that line stretch? To the moon? Maya was at the very front of that line.

With Maya leading the team, the Collins Hill Lady Eagles were nearly unbeatable, winning 125 games and losing only three on the way to three state championships.

And throughout her high school years, Maya proved that a great player could have a good time, too. Basketball is just a game, and games are supposed to be fun. Sometimes coaches, players, and parents forget that. But Maya never did—and she never let her teammates forget, either. Before important games, she kept everyone relaxed in the locker room. She would start a beat, and everyone would clap and dance and sing and sway. When they stepped onto the court, they played free and loose and easy. Other teams could never defeat a team like that!

Even with all the wins and all the fun, Maya never forgot there was more to high school than just basketball. She studied hard, finished her homework on time, spoke up in class, and loved learning new subjects. When she graduated in 2007, she had straight As. Once again, she was at the head of the line.

Seeing her jaw-dropping basketball skills and

high grades, all the best college teams wanted Maya to play for them. After her junior year of high school, she made her decision. She picked UConn, where she knew Coach Auriemma would help her become the best player possible.

CHAPTER FOUR

UCONN FANS KNEW Maya was a special player when she arrived on campus. But did they know she was *this* good? No way. Nobody had ever been *this* good.

She began her first year in 2008 as a backup, spending a lot of time collecting splinters on the bench. But eight games into the season, one of the starters injured her knee. Maya felt bad for her teammate, but she knew this was her chance to show off her skills.

All the sprints, weight lifting, summer camps, and extra practice she'd put in over her entire life had prepared her for this opportunity.

She jumped all over it.

By the end of the season, Maya led the Huskies in scoring, ranked second on the team in rebounds and blocked shots, and placed third in assists. And it wasn't just her stats that impressed her new teammates. She was a hard worker, and she was confident, competitive, and funny. Just like in high school, she invented songs and cheers and everyone else followed along.

None of this was common for a first-year player.

23

When Maya was voted Big East Player of the Year, she became the first person in history—regardless of gender—to win the league's top award as a freshman. And her amazing first season was just the start of an incredible college career stuffed with one accomplishment after another.

Team captain as a sophomore.

National MVP three times.

Academic All-American three times.

All-American all four years of college.

Maya led the Huskies to undefeated seasons in 2009 and 2010, winning national championships both years. In one stretch, UConn won an amazing ninety games in a row. *Sports Illustrated* called her "the greatest winner in the history of women's basketball."

When coaches and teammates described Maya, they used words like "competitive," "determined," "humble," "kind," and "friendly." Even with all her achievements, she never acted like she was better than anyone else. That was because she knew her value as a human being was not defined by her basketball skills and that true happiness did not come from collecting trophies.

Maya knew there were different ways to define "winning." Winning games was one thing. Using basketball to help other people was another. Ever since she was a little kid, she understood that serving others was the most important thing anyone could do in life.

Even as she completed her career at UConn and prepared to play in the WNBA, she hoped her greatest victory in life would come far away from a basketball court.

CHAPTER FIVE

AS A KID in Missouri, Maya was part of the first generation of girls to idolize WNBA players. When she closed her eyes at night, she dreamed of playing in the league someday.

On April 11, 2011, her dream came true. The Minnesota Lynx selected her with the first pick in the WNBA draft.

The only problem was, the Lynx were terrible.

Making it to the WNBA but being picked by the Lynx was like walking into an amazing amusement park—and finding all the rides closed for repairs.

But when Maya arrived, she changed everything for the Lynx.

In her very first season, she was the 2011 WNBA Rookie of the Year and led Minnesota to its first league championship. And she did it again in 2013, 2015, and 2017, teaming with coach Cheryl Reeve and other star players, including Sylvia Fowles and Seimone Augustus, to make the Lynx one of the most powerful dynasties in WNBA history. Maya kept busy in the offseason, too, helping Team USA win gold medals in both the 2012 and

2016 Olympics in London and Rio de Janeiro.

She was officially a worldwide superstar.

Some people thought Maya's life was perfect.

But she knew that wasn't true. After all the excitement of playing college ball at UConn, she was disappointed by the public's lack of enthusiasm for the WNBA.

At UConn, whenever she made a basket, thousands of Huskies fans cheered their hearts out. Just about every game she played was on TV. When she checked into a hotel on a road trip, fans gathered in the lobby to ask for her autograph or pose for a selfie.

But in the WNBA, the energy and excitement fizzled like a punctured basketball. Fans didn't

support women's pro sports the same way they supported men's sports leagues like the NBA. The reasons for this stretched far back in history, all the way to the days when men didn't allow women to compete in the ancient Olympics.

For centuries, courageous women had rebelled against the mistaken idea that women shouldn't sweat or compete or build muscles. But in the world of basketball, women were still playing catch-up. Men's basketball was added to the Olympics in 1936, women's basketball forty years later. The NBA began in 1946, the WNBA not until 1996. Thirty NBA teams played eighty-two games a year; the WNBA had just twelve teams playing only thirty-four games a year (rising to forty in 2023).

WNBA crowds were smaller, and fewer games were televised. Ten times as many people watched the average NBA game on TV as compared to those of the WNBA. The glaring differences frustrated Maya.

"The ball of momentum," Maya said, "is deflating before my eyes."

Still, when she compared her life to the hardships other people experienced, Maya appreciated her good fortune. She was paid to play a game she loved. Success in sports created more opportunities for her to make a difference in the world.

More than ever, Maya understood that she could use her fame to try to make the world a better place.

In 2016, she got her chance.

CHAPTER SIX

IN THE SUMMER of 2016, Maya saw stories on the TV news about two Black men who were unjustly shot and killed by white police officers. The shootings made her sick to her stomach. So before a game on July 9, Maya and three Lynx teammates held a press conference to speak against racism and violence.

Many people admired Maya and her teammates

for talking about something bigger than basketball. Other people said the players should keep their mouths shut, that they were just basketball players, so why did their opinions matter? Maya felt differently. She was a person like anyone else. Her voice did matter. And because she was a basketball star, people paid attention to what she said. She felt a responsibility to use her voice to help others.

But she also believed she needed to do more than just talk.

No one could have predicted how far she was willing to go to prove her point.

On February 6, 2019, after eight years of WNBA stardom, Maya announced she was quitting basketball.

The news shocked her fans. Maya wasn't sick or injured. She wasn't demanding more money. So why was the best player in the world leaving the game in the prime of her career?

The answer was simple. Maya had already achieved everything anyone could dream of in basketball. Now she had something more important to conquer, a secret mission that not many people outside her family knew anything about.

Her best friend was in jail for a crime he did not commit.

His name was Jonathan Irons, and he had been in prison for twenty-one years already, ever since he was eighteen years old. And he wasn't scheduled to be set free for nearly thirty more years.

If life truly was about helping other people, Maya wasn't going to let Jonathan waste away in jail while she dribbled a basketball.

Her whole life, she'd worked as hard as she could to become the world's best basketball player. Now she was going to work even harder to get Jonathan out of prison.

CHAPTER SEVEN

WHEN MAYA FIRST met Jonathan, she was eighteen years old, a high school star about to enroll at UConn.

He was twenty-eight, living behind bars in a small prison cell in Missouri.

The chances that people as different as Maya and Jonathan would ever meet were about as unlikely as a Georgia snowstorm in August.

But one day, in the summer before her first day of college, Maya went on vacation with her family. Her godmother's father, Mr. Flowers, had just met Jonathan in prison, where Mr. Flowers volunteered as the choir director. Jonathan sang in the choir and had a beautiful voice, a great sense of humor, and a warm spirit. Jonathan told Mr. Flowers he didn't belong in prison. He had been sentenced, he said, to fifty years for a crime he did not commit.

Mr. Flowers was no pushover, but he believed Jonathan. And the more Maya learned about the sketchy details of Jonathan's conviction, the more she believed him, too. Maya was someone who always played by the rules. She knew what was right and what was wrong. And she was troubled that an innocent man was locked up in prison. When her godmother asked if she wanted to meet Jonathan, she said yes.

When Jonathan heard that Maya was coming to see him, he wondered why a basketball star would care anything about him. Not many strangers came to see inmates. And when they did, they didn't stay long. Or ever come back.

But when Maya sat across from Jonathan for the first time, she was different than he expected. She looked him in the eyes. She wanted to hear his life story. She treated him with kindness, respect, and patience. She smiled. She treated him as a human being, her equal.

Maya showed Jonathan her competitive side, too. There was a checkerboard in the prison's visiting room. So they played a game.

Maya beat him bad! Jonathan asked for a rematch. Maya said no. She wasn't going to give him another chance.

Not then, anyway. Not until he was out of prison and he could play as a free man.

She wanted him to believe that day would come.

CHAPTER EIGHT

SO HOW DID Jonathan end up in prison, anyway?

One day in January 1997, two police officers ran up to him, tackling him and snapping handcuffs on his wrists. They said a man had been shot and injured by a burglar—and they believed sixteen-year-old Jonathan had done it. They had no evidence, except that someone told them Jonathan was in the neighborhood.

The police wanted Jonathan to confess to the crime. He didn't know what they were talking about; he wasn't the burglar. Alone in a police station, he was a scared kid. But he trusted adults. He figured they would realize they had made a mistake.

But that never happened. Instead, things only got worse.

There were many problems with the case against Jonathan. There was no evidence connecting Jonathan to the crime. No fingerprints, no footprints, no weapon. Still, because he was Black and poor, the odds were stacked against him.

Bryan Stevenson, a well-known lawyer and author who fights against racism, says the justice system

in America "treats you better if you are rich and guilty than if you are poor and innocent."

That's so unfair, but it was exactly the situation facing Jonathan. He didn't have a powerful attorney, and there were no Black people on his jury.

So it was crushing, but not surprising, when the jury found Jonathan guilty. The judge sentenced him to fifty years in prison. He was only sixteen when he was arrested and just eighteen by the end of the trial. Now all he could do was cry. He would be an old man by the time he got out.

His one and only life, he believed, was over.

CHAPTER NINE

ALL THROUGH HER time at UConn and as a star in the WNBA, Maya never forgot about Jonathan. But with her busy schedule, it was hard to find time to talk on the phone. So she wrote him letters. She sent him books. She waved to him when she was on TV. She visited when she could.

Their friendship meant a lot to Jonathan, who felt so lonely. But it was important for Maya, too.

Basketball fans looked up to her like a superhero. She knew she was just a human like anyone else. Staying in touch with Jonathan reminded her of that. As famous and successful as she was, she knew that we're all created equal. We're all in this world together.

Her faith told her to "seek justice, love mercy, and walk humbly."

Fighting for Jonathan's freedom was her way of doing that.

Along with her godparents, Maya searched for any way possible to free Jonathan from prison. There had to be a way to get people to see the truth. And then one day, Maya's godfather discovered a document that had never been shared in court.

CONFIDENTIAL

According to the law, prosecutors are required to turn over evidence that might help the defense. But in Jonathan's case, they never told anyone about a set of fingerprints found in the robbery victim's home that did not belong to Jonathan. If Jonathan could convince a judge to listen to this new information, there was a chance he could be freed from prison. But he needed a lot of help to make his case.

Sadly, there were not many people who cared about Jonathan. This was why Maya had stopped playing basketball when she was the best player in the world: so that she could focus entirely on helping him. She had always been a winner on the basketball court. But freeing Jonathan meant winning in a court of law, and that was a whole new ball game.

CHAPTER TEN

WHILE PREPARING FOR any basketball game, Maya studied her opponent. She learned whether a guard liked to dribble to her left or to her right. She learned whether a team preferred to play man-to-man or zone defense. She knew which players to guard closely and which to let shoot. Preparation was an important part of being a good basketball player.

She approached her work for Jonathan the same way—by studying hard.

She learned that the United States shamefully puts more people in prison than any other country in the world. She learned that because of racism, Black and brown people are locked up at higher rates than white people.

The more Maya learned, the more she wanted other people to understand: Too many people are in prison. Jail sentences are too long. Families and neighborhoods suffer. Jonathan's case inspired her, but she knew many other people needed help, too.

So instead of winning championships, making money, and playing the game she loved, she chose to spend her days helping a man in prison.

Chose to befriend a man who might not breathe free air for decades.

Chose to fight a powerful system.

But the fingerprint evidence her godfather discovered was powerful, too. And a judge was about to make a decision that could change everything for Maya and Jonathan.

CHAPTER ELEVEN

ON MARCH 9, 2020, Maya nervously walked into a small courtroom in Missouri. Jonathan wasn't there. He was sitting in his cell, waiting to hear a decision that might mean freedom—or might doom him to three more decades in prison.

Maya sat in the front row, waiting nervously for the judge to give his opinion.

Maya knew the facts were on Jonathan's side,

but it might not matter. It was hard to win a case like this. The justice system does not like to admit its mistakes.

Taking a seat behind his desk, dressed in a black robe, the judge delivered the news everyone was waiting for. He said it was clear Jonathan had been treated unfairly. Finally, someone with the power to act with mercy and in the interest of justice had done so.

The weight of the world was lifted from Maya's shoulders. She sat quietly with her head buried in her hands, stunned and grateful.

Buzzing with happiness, Maya and her family members walked outside the courtroom to celebrate. Her cell phone rang. It was Jonathan. He

was anxious to know how the judge had ruled.

"Overturned!" Maya exclaimed. "Overturned!"

Overjoyed and overcome with emotion, Jonathan began to sing.

"*Praise the Lord. Hallelujah, I'm free. Hallelujah!*"

CHAPTER TWELVE

IT WOULD TAKE four long months before Maya was finally able to see Jonathan walk out of prison on July 1, 2020.

Maya drove from Atlanta back to Missouri to be there the day Jonathan became a free man. Her long black hair tucked behind a headband, she wore a silver COVID mask, gray sweatpants, and a white T-shirt. With tears in her eyes, she gave

Jonathan a big hug as soon as he walked out the prison doors.

"I feel like I can live life now," he told her. "I'm free; I'm blessed."

Just like that, Jonathan was no longer trapped in the darkness of prison. He was sitting in the passenger seat of Maya's car, a free man riding down the highway. Maya drove Jonathan back to his old neighborhood. Some things looked the same as they had when he was sixteen, but a lot had changed. Maya walked with Jonathan through a cemetery to his grandmother's grave site. When they found her headstone, Jonathan kissed it. "I'm home, Grandma," he said, weeping. "I'm home."

Maya and Jonathan sat down for TV interviews,

telling the world their story and hoping it would inspire other people to work against injustice. Freedom was glorious for Jonathan, and this was a joyful moment for Maya, too, proof that her decision to stop playing basketball at the height of her career had been worth it.

She always believed that she brought more to the world than her basketball skills. Now the people who only knew her as a basketball star understood that, too.

No one knew that more than Jonathan. He admired Maya more than anyone in the world—and that affection had to do with a lot more than basketball. On his second day of freedom, Jonathan dropped to one knee and looked up at

Maya. Their friendship had blossomed into love.

He asked her to marry him. Before he could even finish asking, she said yes.

But it wasn't the end of the story.

CHAPTER THIRTEEN

MAYA AND JONATHAN have been busy since they got married.

They wrote a book about their experience. They started a family, welcoming baby Jonathan Irons Jr. to the world and nicknaming him "JJ."

And they want all of us to think about some important questions.

How do we help other innocent people regain

their freedom? How do we defeat racism? How do we deliver the same justice to poor people as to wealthy people? How do we hold police and attorneys accountable when they don't follow the law?

Maya understands these problems can seem impossible to solve. Not everyone will be able to free an innocent person from prison. Not everyone can quit their career to try.

But everyone can do something. And all those somethings add up.

It might mean speaking with a parent or friend about Maya and Jonathan. It might mean reading books about racism, visiting a courtroom, or helping kids living in poverty. It might be a vote or a donation to a good cause.

It might mean growing up to become a social worker, a teacher, or even a public defender or a thoughtful and honest prosecutor.

You don't have to be a WNBA star to make a difference.

Life is bigger than sports.

Anyone can make a difference.

And everyone should try.

MAYO
CLIN

LEARNING FROM MAYA MOORE: HOW WILL YOU HELP OTHERS?

1. Maya Moore first learned about Jonathan Irons from her godparents.

    - Ask your close friends and family for ideas about injustices they would like to solve or people they would like to help.

2. Maya and Jonathan were from the same hometown of Jefferson City, Missouri.

    - Who are the people in your hometown who are suffering? Are there programs that help those people that you could support?

3. Maya kept supporting Jonathan for years before they won their case in court.

    - Are you willing to work hard for change even if you don't see quick results? What will keep you from quitting when things get hard?

EXTRAS

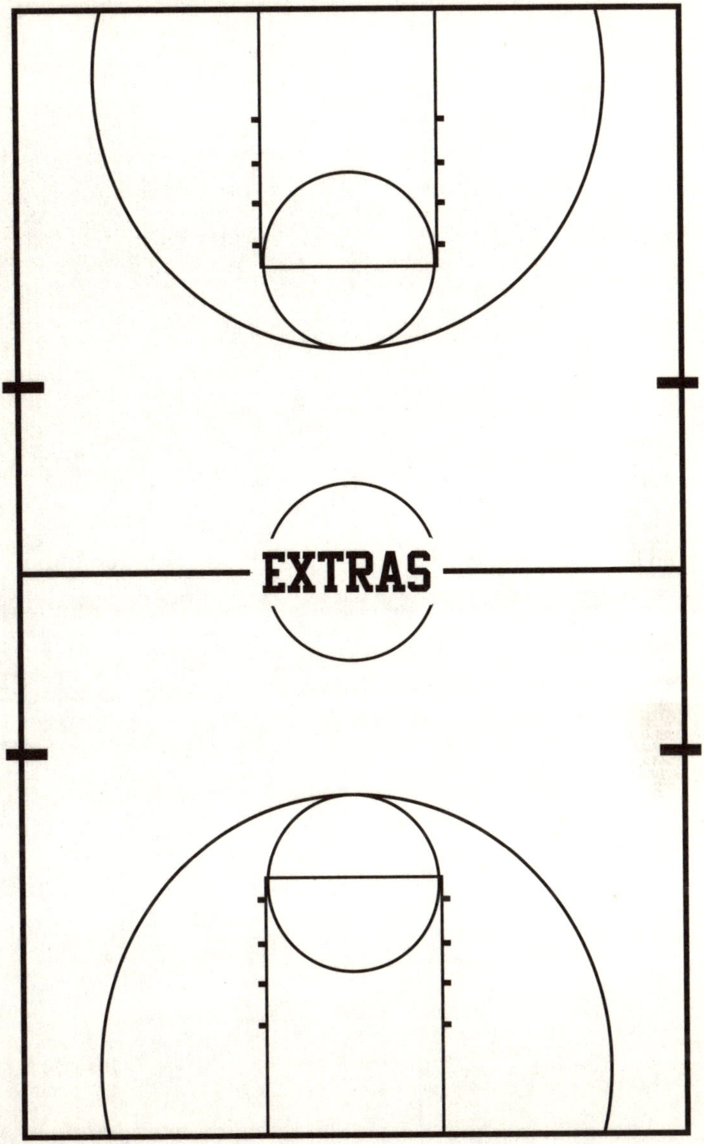

MAYA MOORE UCONN STATISTICS

Year	Age	FT%	FG%	3FG%	APG	SPG	RPG	PPG
2007–08	18	74.3%	54.3%	42.0%	3.1	1.7	7.6	17.8
2008–09	19	78.0%	52.1%	39.8%	3.3	1.9	8.9	19.3
2009–10	20	79.0%	51.5%	41.7%	3.8	2.1	8.3	18.9
2010–11	21	84.3%	52.4%	38.4%	4.0	2.3	8.2	22.8
Career		79.8%	52.5%	40.4%	3.5	2..0	8.3	19.7

*Free Throw Percentage (FT%) * Field Goal Percentage (FG%) * Three-Point Field Goal Percentage (3FG%) * Assists Per Game (APG) * Steals Per Game (SPG) * Rebounds Per Game (RPG) * Points Per Game (PPG)*

MAYA MOORE MINNESOTA LYNX STATISTICS

Year	Age	FT%	FG%	3FG%	APG	SPG	RPG	PPG
2011	22	78.8%	43.9%	36.9%	2.6	1.4	4.6	13.2
2012	23	87.9%	46.5%	38.8%	3.6	1.5	6.0	16.4
2013	24	88.2%	50.9%	45.3%	3.0	1.7	6.2	18.5
2014	25	88.4%	48.1%	33.5%	3.4	1.9	8.1	23.9
2015	26	85.5%	42.0%	35.9%	3.5	1.7	6.7	20.6
2016	27	86.8%	44.8%	40.4%	4.2	1.6	5.1	19.3
2017	28	85.8%	44.2%	41.1%	3.5	1.9	5.0	17.3
2018	29	83.3%	42.3%	36.5%	2.6	1.7	5.1	18.0
Career		86.0%	45.3%	38.4%	3.3	1.7	5.9	18.4

2012 AND 2016 OLYMPICS

Year	Site	Gold	Silver	Bronze	Maya's PPG	Maya's RPG	Maya's APG
2012	London	USA	France	Australia	9.0	5.6	2.6
2016	Rio	USA	Spain	Serbia	12.0	5.6	4.3

NCAA AND WNBA CHAMPION AND RUNNER-UP DURING MAYA'S CAREER

	NCAA		WNBA	
Year	Champion	Runner-Up	Champion	Runner-Up
2008	Tennessee	Stanford	Detroit Shock	San Antonio Silver Stars
2009	**UConn**	Louisville	Phoenix Mercury	Indiana Fever
2010	**UConn**	Stanford	Seattle Storm	Atlanta Dream
2011	Texas	Notre Dame	**Minnesota Lynx**	Atlanta Dream
2012	Baylor	Notre Dame	Indiana Fever	**Minnesota Lynx**
2013	UConn	Louisville	**Minnesota Lynx**	Atlanta Dream
2014	UConn	Notre Dame	Phoenix Mercury	Chicago Sky
2015	UConn	Notre Dame	**Minnesota Lynx**	Indiana Fever
2016	UConn	Syracuse	Los Angeles Sparks	**Minnesota Lynx**
2017	South Carolina	Mississippi State	**Minnesota Lynx**	Los Angeles Sparks
2018	Notre Dame	Mississippi State	Seattle Storm	Washington Mystics

*Maya's teams bolded**

WADE TROPHY MULTIPLE-TIME WINNERS

NAME	SCHOOL	YEAR
Nancy Lieberman	Old Dominion	1979 1980
Seimone Augustus	LSU	2005 2006
Maya Moore	UConn	2009 2010 2011
Brittney Griner	Baylor	2012 2013
Breanna Stewart	UConn	2015 2016
Sabrina Ionescu	Oregon	2019 2020

TOP 10 WORLD PRISON POPULATIONS

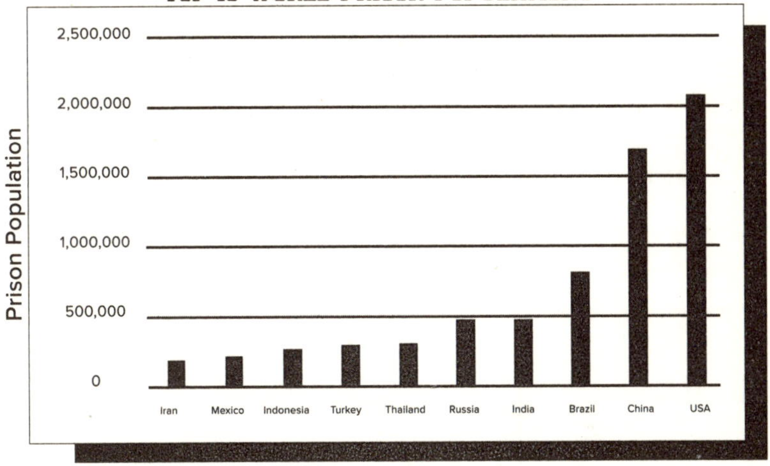

TOP 10 HIGHEST WORLD INCARCERATION RATES

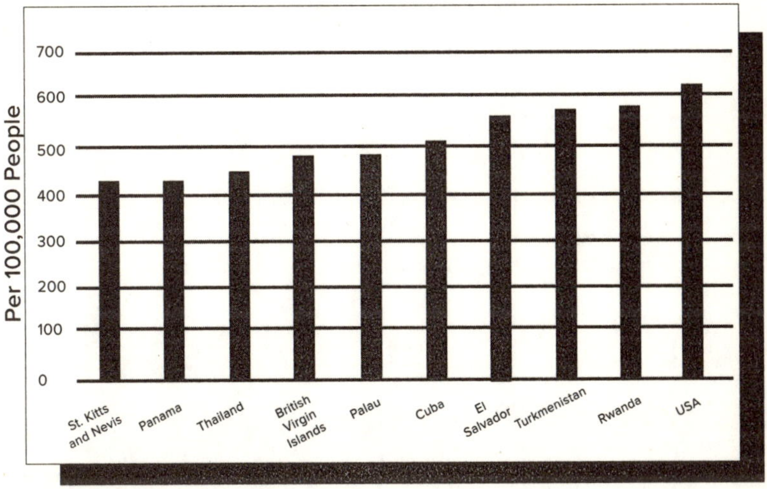

World Prison Brief, 2021.

GLOSSARY

All-American: An athlete honored as one of the best amateurs in the US.

conviction: A ruling that someone is guilty of a crime, made by a jury verdict or a judge's decision.

criminal justice system: The system of law enforcement involved in apprehending, prosecuting, defending, sentencing, and punishing those suspected or convicted of crimes.

defendant: An individual accused in a court of law.

defense attorney: A lawyer representing someone accused of a crime.

evidence: Information presented to a court of law to help determine the truth of a situation.

exoneration: The act of clearing someone of a criminal charge.

jury: People (jurors) sworn to give a verdict in a legal case based on evidence submitted in court.

mass incarceration: Refers to the extreme rates of imprisonment in the US and the concentration of imprisonment among young Black men.

prosecutor: A lawyer who conducts the case against a defendant in a criminal court.

prosecutor-initiated resentencing: A method for prosecutors to look back at unjust, excessive sentences and bring people back to their families and communities.

restorative justice: A system that focuses on the rehabilitation of offenders through reconciliation with victims and the community.

sentence: The punishment given by a court of law.

vacated conviction: A guilty verdict that is withdrawn by a court, effectively dismissing the charges against someone convicted of a crime.

wrongful conviction: A conviction may be classified as "wrongful" for two reasons:

1. The person convicted is factually innocent of the charges.
2. There were procedural errors that violated the convicted person's rights.

RESOURCES FOR FAMILIES

- Equal Justice Initiative: EJI.org
- Impact Justice: ImpactJustice.org
- Innocence Project: InnocenceProject.org
- National Registry of Exonerations: Law.UMich .edu/Special/Exoneration
- The Sentencing Project: SentencingProject.org
- WNBA: WNBA.com

- Watch the *Breakaway* documentary on Maya and Jonathan on ESPN+.
- Read Maya's essay on stepping away from the sport of basketball on the Players' Tribune website.
- Read coverage of her efforts to free Jonathan by Kurt Streeter in *The New York Times* and by Katie Barnes on ESPN.com.
- Watch interviews with Maya and Jonathan conducted by Robin Roberts of ABC.
- Visit the Equal Justice Initiative's Legacy Museum in Montgomery, Alabama.

AUTHOR BIO

ANDREW MARANISS writes nonfiction books about sports and social justice for children, teens, and adults. His first *New York Times* bestselling adult book, *Strong Inside*, received the Lillian Smith Book Award for civil rights and the RFK Book Awards' Special Recognition Prize for social justice. The Young Readers adaptation of *Strong Inside* was named a Book of the Year by the American Library Association. Andrew's second book, the YA narrative nonfiction *Games of Deception*, received the Sydney Taylor Book Honor. His third book, the YA biography *Singled Out*, was named one of the 100 Best Baseball Books Ever Written by *Esquire* magazine. His latest book, *Inaugural Ballers*, tells the story of the first US women's Olympic basketball team. Andrew manages special projects at the Vanderbilt University athletic department, including the university's Sports and Society Initiative. He lives in Nashville with his wife and two young children. Follow him on Twitter @TruBlu24 and at AndrewMaraniss.com.

READ MORE IN THE

Beyond THE GAME SERIES!

AVAILABLE NOW!

AND STAY TUNED FOR WHATS NEXT:

Beyond THE GAME

ATHLETES CHANGE THE WORLD

PAT TILLMAN

COMING IN THE FALL OF 2024!